VISUALIZE
YOUR
PROFESSIONAL
FUTURE

VISUALIZE YOUR PROFESSIONAL FUTURE

A Framework for Mapping Aspirations to Achieve Career Success

KERRON DUNCAN & DR. MALIKA GRAYSON-DUNCAN

To purchase books in bulk, please contact the publisher.

Mynd Matters Publishing
2690 Cobb Parkway SE, Ste A5-375, Smyrna, GA 30080
888-833-2548
www.myndmatterspublishing.com

ISBN: 978-1-963874-45-7 (pbk)
ISBN: 978-1-963874-56-3 (hdcv)

FIRST EDITION

This workbook is dedicated to the dreamers, the planners, and the doers—the ones who dare to envision their ultimate aspirations and take intentional steps to make it a reality. May this resource empower you to create a career and life that align with your passions, values, and purpose.

Who Should Use This Workbook?

We have all asked ourselves, *What's next in my career journey?* In a rapidly changing professional landscape, the need for clarity, purpose, and forward-thinking has never been more essential. Whether just starting a career or having years of experience, we all reach a point where we begin the cycle of thinking about our progress—whether it be progress towards short-term goals or long-term goals. However, it's insufficient to merely lay out our goals and aspirations. Equally crucial is implementing an action plan that aligns these visualizations of our desires with high-level goals that can then be used to systematically translate them into manageable, actionable, and achievable steps. Throughout these pages, we will walk through how to navigate the intersection of vision and action confidently.

What You Will Learn

This workbook is a resource for anyone discovering how to make their career dreams a reality through purposeful planning. These pages explore the skill of balancing your current path with forward-looking aspirations, a crucial step in visualizing career ambitions. It also includes the steps to craft a career vision board—a tool that empowers individuals to crystallize their ambitions, set clear objectives, and forge a well-defined path toward success.

In this workbook, you will:

- Understand the significance of visualizing career aspirations.
- Learn how to select meaningful images, words, and affirmations that align with career aspirations to build a career vision board.
- Explore the need to implement an action plan to bridge the gap between visualized aspirations and high-level career objectives.
- Discover practical strategies for turning career aspirations into actionable tasks through systematic goal planning.
- Learn how to evaluate progress by using success indicators to measure achievements and refine your goals.

Contents

Introduction

There is a story about a sailor navigating a vast ocean without a map or compass. At first, it seems manageable - the sailor can rely on the wind and currents, adjusting course with instinct alone. But as the days stretch into weeks, the endless horizon becomes disorienting. Without a clear destination or guide, every direction starts to feel the same, and soon, the sailor is simply drifting.

Now imagine that sailor being handed a map, a carefully drawn chart, that not only identifies a destination but also highlights key landmarks, constellations and routes. Suddenly, the journey transforms and there is purpose. Each wave is no longer an obstacle but part of a larger plan. Each gust of wind becomes an opportunity to move forward. The sailor begins to move with clarity and intention, confidently steering toward their goal.

Our careers are much like that sailor's journey across the ocean—that vast global industry to which we each belong. Without a clear vision of where we want to go, we risk drifting—feeling lost, unsure, and reactive rather than intentional. Yet, when we take the time to visualize our professional future and create a clear plan, we gain direction and purpose. That visualization becomes our compass, and a well-structured plan becomes our map, guiding us through challenges, helping us seize opportunities, and keeping us on course toward achieving our dreams.

The Power of Visualization and Action

This workbook is a tool to help you take control of your career path. It's about moving from a place of uncertainty to one of clarity, confidence, and purpose. Visualization is not just wishful thinking. It's a powerful method for creating a mental blueprint of your goals and aspirations. Research shows that when we visualize success, we engage our subconscious minds in ways that improve focus, motivation, and problem-solving.

However, visualization alone is not enough. Dreams without action remain fantasies. What is your ultimate aspiration? Have you taken steps toward it? This workbook bridges the gap between envisioning your professional future and taking the necessary steps to make it a reality. It will guide you to transform your career dreams into actionable goals and equip you with practical strategies and tools to craft a clear and effective roadmap.

What This Workbook Will Do for You

This workbook is your guide for translating career aspirations into tangible outcomes. It will take you on a journey from **visualization to realization** by helping you:

- Reflect deeply on where you are and where you want to go.
- Crystallize your ambitions into a clear vision and actionable plan.
- Discover the transformative power of visualization techniques, such as crafting a vision board and creating a vision statement.
- Translate high-level aspirations into measurable objectives and step-by-step action plans.
- Stay inspired, grounded, and focused throughout your career.

Each chapter introduces concepts, tools, and resources to turn your career aspirations into realities:

Chapter 1: Visualizing Your Career Aspirations – In this chapter, we begin with reflections, an exercise in the power of visualization and self-reflection as we envision the future as the starting point for defining our professional future and paths towards achieving that future. Why is this necessary? Self-reflections on our current career path and future state of success, *our aspirations*, are required for us to gain clarity on the direction to pursue, setting the stage for the path ahead.

Chapter 2: Building a Career Vision Board – Next, we will bring our career aspirations to life visually through a tangible and creative process. Vision boards help us anchor our goals in a meaningful and clear format meant to inspire, reignite our drive, and guide our focus on the course to making those aspirations a reality.

Chapter 3: Crafting Your Vision Statement – From the vision board as the foundation, we will shape a concise vision statement that captures the essence of where you want to go in your career. This statement may serve as a beacon as it aligns with your values and dreams and helps you navigate as you stay aligned to your long-term ambitions.

Chapter 4: Defining Career Vision Goals – In this chapter, we will take the vision board and vision statement and break them down to high level strategic goals. These goals can serve as milestones that bring clarity, helping you to track progress and stay committed to the larger vision.

Chapter 5: From Goals to Objectives –We will focus on using the goals that have been outlined to set realistic and measurable objectives that support those career vision goals. These objectives provide a roadmap through the steps of your professional growth, turning the aspirations from the first chapter into actions and eventual achievements. We will then implement these objectives by developing an action plan. By using actionable steps, support systems and being persistent you can confidently bring the vision to life.

Chapter 6: Bringing It All Together – We will focus on the key lessons from the previous chapters, transforming aspirations into a structured roadmap for career success. In this chapter we will reinforce the importance of execution, accountability, and adaptability, ensuring that vision, goals, and SMART objectives translate into meaningful progress.

Chapter 7: Sustaining Momentum – Success is not just about achieving goals but about continuously evolving, adapting, and staying resilient through career changes. This chapter emphasizes the importance of maintaining motivation, reassessing goals, and proactively managing career transitions. We will explore strategies for overcoming setbacks, future-proofing your career, and leveraging your network to stay relevant in a changing professional landscape. With a focus on growth, adaptability, and long-term vision, this chapter ensures that your career journey remains intentional, strategic, and fulfilling.

Why This Matters

In today's fast-paced professional landscape, the ability to set a clear career path is more critical than ever. Whether you are a recent graduate, a mid-career professional, or someone contemplating a significant shift, this workbook is for you. It's designed to help you take control of your narrative, harness your unique potential, and pursue your goals with intention.

As the world we live in continues to evolve rapidly and opportunities often feel fleeting, a structured approach to career planning has never been more critical. The uncertainty of career paths can be daunting, but this workbook empowers you to take control. Remember, it's not about predicting the future, it's about preparing for it.

By the time you finish this workbook, you will have more than just a vision for your career, you will also have a concrete action plan that transforms aspirations into achievements. Consider this workbook your co-pilot, a trusted resource to navigate the twists and turns of your career and guide you toward the professional future you have always imagined.

Your Career, Your Map, Your Journey

Your career is a story waiting to be written, and this framework is the tool to help you write it with purpose and precision. As you work through the chapters, you will gain clarity about what you truly want, courage to dream bigger, and confidence to take the steps necessary to turn those dreams into reality.

So, let's begin. Let's draw the map of your professional future, navigate the vast ocean of possibilities, and move forward with boldness and intention toward the career of your dreams. As you review each chapter, keep in mind that the section and exercises in this workbook cannot be rushed and will take time. Some exercises such as drafting the career vision statement will take more time or multiple efforts. This is the iterative process that must be followed to ensure there is clarity as you complete each step.

CHAPTER 1

Envisioning Your Future: A Journey of Self-Discovery

"Where there is no vision, the people perish."
—Proverbs 29:18 KJV

Aspirations serve as a guiding compass, helping us navigate personal growth and reach our fullest potential. This chapter focuses on your pathway of self-discovery, where you will transform your career desires into a compelling vision for your future.

Vision is an intentional creation, born from reflection, self-awareness, and commitment. Before crafting yours, it is essential to explore your identity, inspiration, and how your aspirations align with your purpose. This process will serve as the foundation for transforming your dreams into a concrete roadmap for your future. Throughout this chapter, we will unravel the complex tapestry of personal aspirations.

You will learn to:

- Identify the core desires, strengths and aspirations that resonate with your values through self-reflection.
- Navigate and discover trends, shifts in your field and other factors that can be accelerants or disruptors in your vision.
- Develop a vision framework for translating abstract dreams into a concrete definition of your future self.
- Understand the powerful connection between belief and achievement.

In this chapter we will delve deeper into the process of self-reflection and self-assessments, tap into the creative spirit of vision board creation, and craft vision statements, goals and objectives that resonate. All of these are critical in laying a firm foundation and roadmap for continually evolving your career plan during potential disruption and challenges.

We will also explore the fundamental building blocks of personal and professional growth. This will allow us to examine aspirations as a driving force, identifying and overcoming limitations, and conducting a comprehensive self-assessment. By engaging in this process with intentionality, you will gain the clarity needed to craft a vision that is not only ambitious but deeply aligned with your values and purpose. By the end of this chapter, you will have greater clarity on your motivations, a framework for transforming your aspirations into an actionable vision, and practical strategies for sustained personal growth. This road to self-discovery sets the stage for Chapter 2, where you will create your vision board and bring your future into focus.

Through structured exercises and thought-provoking questions, you will:

- Define your aspirations and understand their role in shaping your career path
- Identify and challenge self-imposed limitations that may be holding you back
- Conduct a personal assessment to map out your strengths, growth areas, and opportunities
- Gain deeper insight into what inspires and fuels your passion

This foundational work will equip you with the tools to design a vision that is both bold and achievable. This transformative process begins by first understanding the power of aspirations and their role in shaping your path forward.

Understanding Aspirations: The Fuel of Personal Transformation

Aspirations are more than simple wishes or fleeting dreams. They are profound connections to our deepest values, purpose, and potential. These intrinsic motivators serve as powerful catalysts that propel us forward, especially when faced with challenges, setbacks, or moments of uncertainty.

Think of aspirations as an internal compass, guiding us through complex life decisions, unexpected challenges, and periods of uncertainty while helping us stay steadfast in our purpose. Aspirations empower us to:

- Navigate difficult and complex decisions
- Maintain resilience in the face of adversity
- Align our actions with our most authentic self
- Make meaningful progress toward our most significant goals

As Oprah Winfrey eloquently stated, "Create the highest, grandest vision possible for your life, because you become what you believe."

Crafting a vision is one of the most powerful subconscious actions we can take to ignite the creative process and bring that vision to life. Once you begin, you will naturally be drawn to self-reflection by assessing how your vision aligns with your current reality and identifying the gaps that must be bridged. From there, the focus shifts to acceleration: What steps will propel you forward? What support do you need? How can you ensure you are moving in the right direction? And crucially, how do you prepare for inevitable disruptions? To help answer these questions, we have established five core tenets that serve as the foundation for successfully providing the clarity, direction, and resilience needed to turn vision into reality.

Aspirations alone are not enough. Self-reflection bridges the gap between dreams and action. This process will help you recognize your strengths, challenges, and the areas where you need to grow. By looking inward, you gain clarity on how to turn your aspirations into an actionable vision.

Self-Reflection

Self-reflection is a fundamental and essential practice that we will refine throughout. In an ever-evolving landscape of business, technology, and society, self-reflection is not a one-time exercise but a continuous, strategic process. Successful individuals and organizations consistently iterate, recalibrate, and realign their actions with their vision and purpose. As we progress, self-reflection will serve as a critical foundation for developing a vision board, crafting a compelling vision statement, setting tangible goals, and taking purposeful action.

Unlocking the Power of Vision: The Five Tenets of Transformation

Transformation isn't just about dreaming, it requires action. The five tenets introduced here will help you craft a bold vision, strengthen your mindset, and take purposeful steps toward your goals. Each tenet challenges conventional boundaries, fueling the belief and strategies needed to turn your aspirations into reality.

Let's explore how each tenet helps you create with intention, imagine audaciously, believe unwaveringly, and push past barriers to transformation.

1. Intentional Creation

A vision is not accidental. It must be deliberately and proactively crafted with purpose and intention. Visions require active planning, reflection, and strategic thinking to ensure every decision is a conscious choice that shapes your path, and your own personal agency is crucial in enabling your success. Intentional Creation ensures that every step you take is aligned with your values, strengths, and long-term vision. It helps you focus on what truly matters, eliminating distractions and uncertainty by providing a structured path forward.

2. Audacious Imagination

Your vision should stretch beyond comfortable boundaries, representing the most ambitious version of yourself. This is an opportunity for you to challenge existing mental models of your future and envision possibilities beyond your current skills, expertise, or capabilities. It is a moment to break free from societal and even self-imposed restrictions, gradually building confidence by pursuing increasingly ambitious goals, dreaming bigger than what seems immediately possible. When you give yourself permission to dream big, you open the door to groundbreaking opportunities and innovative solutions that redefine your career and life.

3. Transformative Belief

Beliefs are powerful architects of our reality, shaping perceptions, decisions, and outcomes. When you believe in your potential, you unlock the confidence to act—and action drives success. It is a force that generates the energy and momentum needed to thrive in times of change and disruption. Doubt, fear, and uncertainty can often hold us back, but a strong belief in your vision and capabilities will propel you forward, even when faced with obstacles. Transformation is not just about setting goals, it's about having the resilience and confidence to navigate setbacks and continuously push toward growth. When you truly believe in your potential, you cultivate the mindset necessary to turn setbacks into lessons, challenges into opportunities, and uncertainty into possibility.

4. Interconnected Synthesis

These principles work together as a powerful framework for personal transformation. The journey ahead is not just about setting goals, it's about redefining how you think, plan, and act in pursuit of a future that aligns with your highest aspirations. The exercises, questions, and activities in this workbook are designed to help you internalize and apply these principles in a way that fuels meaningful change. You have the power to consciously design your future, to imagine possibilities beyond limitations, and to believe in your ability to make them a reality. Ahead lies a path of empowerment, action, and transformation, and it begins with the decision to step fully into your potential.

5. Breaking Through Limitations

Breaking through limitations, whether self-imposed, societal, or deeply ingrained, is crucial to realizing your vision. Many people find themselves constrained by self-imposed limitations, societal expectations, or deeply ingrained beliefs about what is truly possible. This chapter provides strategic tools to help you proactively address skill gaps and cultivate a growth mindset in your career. A growth mindset is where we change our perspective from focusing on what we can't accomplish to realizing that all things are possible with training, practice, and with support from others in our network. Creating a personalized approach to overcoming challenges can also help you become successful by applying your unique strengths and experiences to any challenge you may face. Continual application of your strengths, growth of your skills, and success can help you build resilience as you pursue your aspirations. Now, let's begin the self-assessment journey by lighting the path to uncover the strengths and building blocks already within you to bring your vision to life.

The Self-Assessment Journey

The foundation of a clear vision begins with self-reflection, understanding your aspirations, overcoming limitations, and assessing the experiences that have shaped you. Identifying what fuels your passion and drives your sense of purpose is the first step toward defining a compelling and actionable vision. Recognizing what gives you fulfillment will help shape a vision that is both meaningful and motivating.

Beyond internal passion, external experiences play a significant role in shaping who you are. Defining moments, both struggles and victories, influence how you see the world and how you show up in your career and life. Whether it's people who have inspired you, challenges that pushed you to grow, or pivotal lessons that now guide your leadership and decision-making, acknowledging these influences provides valuable insight.

Equally important is understanding your impact and the legacy you want to leave behind. By recognizing the influence you have had so far, you can refine your vision with intention, ensuring that your aspirations align with the broader impact you seek to make.

Identifying What Inspires You

This section will help you uncover what fuels your curiosity, energizes you, and shapes your aspirations. Through guided questions, you will be able to pinpoint your core passions, motivations, and defining moments.

There are several ways for us to assess your passions but the approach we're taking is to walk through a set of brief exercises. The full exercise will take about 90 minutes to complete and will focus on three core sections.

The first exercise is about what fuels your inner fire. These are the passions, values, and beliefs that energize you, the things that spark excitement and make you eager to start each day. It's what gives you a deep sense of purpose and fulfillment.

In the second exercise, we will explore is how external forces have shaped you and have become your defining moments. These experiences, both struggles and victories, have influenced how you see the world. It could be the people who have inspired or challenged you to grow, or the lessons you have learned that now guide how you lead, work, and show up every day.

The third exercise is about understanding your impact and defining your bigger purpose. It's about the problems you want to solve, the changes you strive to create, and how you aim to shape the future, whether in your industry, community, or the world. Ultimately, it's about the legacy you want to leave behind based on how you have impacted your environment to date, your strengths and interests. This will be a great segway into creating your vision board.

Exercise 1: Your Inner Fire – What Fuels You?

Purpose: This exercise is designed to help you uncover the passions, values, and beliefs that fuel your motivation and sense of purpose. This exercise encourages deep reflection on what truly excites and energizes you, helping you identify the core drivers behind your ambitions and aspirations. Understanding your Inner Fire will ensure that the goals you set are not just about professional success but also about deep personal satisfaction and purpose-driven impact.

Before we dive into the exercises, here are a couple of tools to help you think through the professionally aligned activities that bring you joy and fuel your passions. Listed below is a table of potential passions aligned to a list of activities. A second table listing examples of values is also added for your consideration.

Table 1: Passion and Activities

Passion Area	Example Activities
Culinary Arts	Cooking, baking, food tasting, mixology
Craftsmanship & Building	Woodworking, pottery, sewing, DIY projects
Lifestyle & Wellness	Fitness, meditation, travel, spirituality
Creative Arts	Writing, photography, music, dance, theater
Business & Entrepreneurship	Starting a business, networking, investing
Animal Care & Nature	Pet care, wildlife conservation, botany
Education & Teaching	Tutoring, teaching, content creation
Technology	Coding, video game development, robotics
Physical & Outdoor Activities	Sports, hiking, gardening, yoga
Academic & Intellectual Pursuits	History, philosophy, languages, math
Social & Community Activities	Activism, volunteering, mentoring

Table 2: Core Values

Core Value	Definition
Honesty	Truthfulness in words and actions.
Integrity	Doing what is right, even when it's difficult or unseen.
Resilience	Bouncing back from challenges and adversity.
Adaptability	Flexibility and openness to change.
Accountability	Taking ownership of responsibilities and outcomes.
Empathy	Understanding and sharing others' feelings and perspectives.
Courage	Willingness to take risks and face fears.
Respect	Valuing people, boundaries, and differing views.
Discipline	Consistency, focus, and self-regulation.
Growth	Pursuit of learning and continuous improvement.
Gratitude	Appreciation for people, experiences, and opportunities.
Open-mindedness	Receptiveness to new ideas and perspectives.
Confidence	Self-belief and assurance in one's abilities.
Purpose	Having direction and intention behind your actions.

Core Value	Definition
Creativity	Original thinking and innovation.
Service	Helping others and contributing to the greater good.
Leadership	Inspiring and guiding individuals or groups toward a goal.

Activity A: The Power Surge – What Gives You Energy?   Time: 10 min

Set a timer for two minutes per question. Spend no more than the two minutes allotted on each question. For each question, write your gut reaction answers. Do not overthink it, just go with whatever pops into your head.

What is one passion or activity you could talk about for hours without getting bored?

_____

_____

_____

_____

Think of an occasion when you were so engaged in an activity that you lost track of time. What were you doing?

_____

_____

_____

_____

If your schedule magically cleared up tomorrow, what's the first passion or activity you would want to do?

_____

_____

_____

_____

Now, look at your answers. What themes stand out?

_____

_____

_____

_____

_____

_____

_____

_____

_____

_____

_____

_____

Activity B: Your Inner Fire in One Sentence – What Drives You?   Time: 10 min

Use your answers from Activity A to complete the sentence below. Use the list of passions, activities and values provided earlier in the chapter to help you fill in the sentence.

"I am most energized when I [activity or impact] because I believe in [core value]. My fire is fueled by [passion], and I am driven to [bigger purpose]."

Workspace: Fill in your activity, core value, passion and purpose below.

"I am most energized when I _____ **because I believe in** _____**."**

"My fire is fueled by _____**, and I am driven to** _____**."**

Bonus Challenge   Time: 2 min

If you had to describe your **inner fire in ONE word**, what would it be?

_____

Write it down and keep it with you as a daily reminder.

In conclusion, this exercise is more than just an exploration of your passion, it is a foundation for intentional and fulfilling growth. By identifying what truly excites and motivates you, you create a guiding compass for your career and life decisions. When challenges arise, reconnecting with your inner fire will help you stay focused, resilient, and inspired. As you move forward in this workbook, let this newfound clarity serve as a powerful anchor, ensuring that every step you take aligns with your deepest values and long-term aspirations.

Exercise 2: Defining Moments – External Forces That Shaped You

Purpose: We all have experiences, both challenges and victories that have shaped the way we think, work, and lead. These defining moments influence how we approach problems, make decisions, and show up in the world. Some experiences push us to grow, while others teach us valuable lessons that stay with us for life.

This exercise will help you reflect on the key experiences, people, and lessons that have influenced you. By understanding how these moments have shaped you, you can harness their power to drive your growth, leadership, and future success.

Activity A: Defining Moments – What Shaped You?   Time: 10 min

This is also a quick reflection round. Set a timer for two minutes per question. <u>Spend no more than the two minutes allotted on each question.</u>

Think of one professional or personal achievement that made you feel unstoppable:

_____

_____

Think of one challenge or setback that taught you a valuable lesson:

_____

_____

Who or what has influenced the way you lead, work, or show up in the world?

_____

_____

Look for patterns in your responses. What moments have had the biggest impact on shaping who you are?

_____

_____

Activity B: Defining Moments Timeline   Time: 15 min

Use the timeline below to mark 3-5 moments in your life that have had a lasting impact on you and then briefly describe why the event was impactful. Classify each as either challenge, win or moment of influence. Also keep in mind that the defining moment could be a conversation with a person, a tough challenge, or a moment of clarity that had a lasting impact on your life.

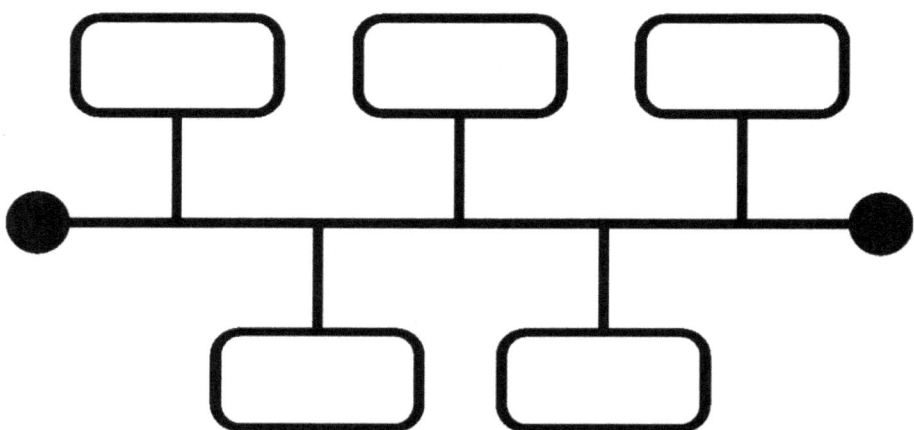

Defining Moment #1

Event Title: _____   *Age or Year:* _____

Describe the Event:

_____

_____

_____

How does this moment still impact you today?

_____

_____

_____

Defining Moment #2

Event Title: _____   *Age or Year:* _____

Describe the Event:

_____

_____

_____

How does this moment still impact you today?

_____

_____

_____

Defining Moment #3

Event Title: _____   *Age or Year:* _____

Describe the Event:

_____

_____

_____

How does this moment still impact you today?

_____

_____

_____

Defining Moment #4

Event Title: _____   *Age or Year:* _____

Describe the Event:

_____

_____

_____

How does this moment still impact you today?

_____

_____

_____

Defining Moment #5

Event Title: _____   *Age or Year:* _____

Describe the Event:

_____

_____

_____

How does this moment still impact you today?

_____

_____

_____

Summarizing Defining Moments

Now, let's summarize our defining moments into a summary sentence using the template below.

"My experiences have taught me [add core lessons]

_____

_____

_____

_____

_____

_____

"Because [add key defining moments],

_____

_____

_____

_____

I now [add how you apply it to your life/work]

_____

_____

_____

_____

By identifying these defining moments, you gain insight into how past experiences influence how you solve problems, navigate adversity, and show up in the world. Some moments push you to grow, while others leave lessons that shape your values and purpose. This reflection will help you better understand the external forces that have molded you, providing clarity as you move forward in your personal and professional life.

Exercise 3: Defining Your Impact & Legacy – The Mark You Leave

Purpose: This exercise helps define your strengths and the impact you want to make. Reflecting on past contributions and future aspirations will clarify the legacy you want to build and help begin the foundation for your vision board.

Activity A: Looking Back – Your Strengths and Impact   Time: 10 min

Set a timer for two minutes per question. <u>Spend no more than the two minutes allotted on each question.</u> Remember, do not overthink it.

What are 2-3 meaningful contributions you have made in your career, community, or personal life?

_____

_____

_____

_____

What 3-4 strengths have allowed you to make an impact?

_____

_____

_____

_____

Who has benefited from your actions, leadership, or expertise?

_____

_____

_____

_____

What challenges have you helped solve or improve?

_____

_____

_____

_____

How have people described your influence or impact (feel free to ask someone who knows you well)?

_____

_____

_____

_____

Activity B: Looking Ahead – The Change You Want to Create   Time: 10 min

Set a timer for two minutes per question. Reflect on your future aspirations using the following questions.

What are the biggest challenges in your industry or community that you feel passionate about addressing?

_____

_____

_____

How do your strengths and interests align with solving these problems?

_____

_____

_____

If you had unlimited resources, what problem would you solve first?

_____

_____

_____

What kind of change do you want to be known for driving?

_____

_____

_____

Who do you want to uplift, empower, or inspire?

_____

_____

_____

Activity C: Your Legacy Statement – Defining Your Purpose   **Time: 10 min**

Summarize your reflections into a powerful purpose statement—one or two sentences that describe the impact you want to have and the mark you want to leave on the world.

Example:

"I am committed to driving innovation in technology and mentoring the next generation of diverse leaders, ensuring the future is shaped by inclusion, automation, and transformation. My legacy will be one of breaking barriers, fostering growth, and creating opportunities for those who come after me."

Write your impact statement below:

_____

_____

_____

_____

_____

_____

This exercise is designed to help you reflect on your strengths, past contributions, and the impact you have made so far. By examining the problems you want to solve and the changes you strive to create, you will gain deeper insight into your higher purpose. Understanding how your strengths and interests align with your aspirations will provide a strong foundation for shaping your vision board, ensuring that your future goals are rooted in meaningful impact and purpose. With your aspirations and defining moments in mind, let's bring your vision to life. In the next chapter, you will create a vision board - a tangible blueprint for your future.

CHAPTER 2

Creating a Career Vision Board

"Vision animates, inspires, transforms purpose into action."
—Warren G. Bennis

The Power of Visualization in Achieving Success

What does success look like to you? Whatever success means to you, visualizing your success is the first step to making it real. Have you ever noticed how clearly visualizing something makes it feel more achievable? Researchers have found that visualization can optimize performance by activating the same areas of the brain as the actual experience. This mental "programming" helps individuals overcome challenges and achieve their goals more effectively [1]. In their research, they found that mental imagery can significantly enhance performance, motivation, and goal attainment. It is commonly said that the practice of visualization contributes to career success and achievements.

In sports, visualization is used to improve sports performance by visualizing the specified skills and strategies, activating neural pathways. This mental imagery is intended to mimic physical performance [2]. Just as athletes use visualization to sharpen their skills, professionals can harness the same power to manifest career success. Creating a career vision board programs your subconscious mind to focus on achieving professional milestones. Now, let's transition from Chapter 1, where we explored aspirations to visualizing them through a career vision board. This chapter is an important step in realizing our career aspirations by creating a visual and tangible tool.

Bringing Your Career Aspirations to Life

When we think of the term "vision board," we think of a collage or visual representation of all that inspires and motivates us as we reflect on our desires and dreams that we want to accomplish during a specified time period [3]. Usually, those images are aspirational, a source of inspiration and almost euphoric as we are filled with excitement on the journey that lies ahead, and we think about "end game." End game being the visual representation we have physically created to remind us of where we would like to be. However, a vision board isn't just about the goals and desires we have visually represented, it is about the actions we need to take to get to *our version* of that visual. The actions to get there will be tackled in a later section but first, we need to complete the visual representation since that will lead to understanding the actions we must take to be on the path towards our goals and desires. Vision boards are powerful tools and tangible representations for manifesting our desires and goals. Simply, they are a strategic tool we can use to help us transform dreams into reality by clarifying goals, enhancing focus, and motivating us through visual reinforcement.

When it comes to crafting a career vision board, the process becomes more targeted and strategic, guiding us towards our professional objectives.

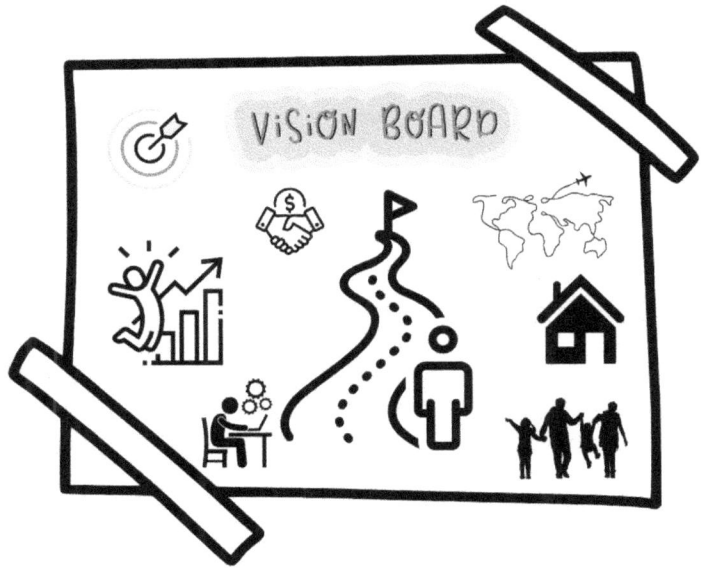

Vision Boards: Personal vs. Career

Before diving into the specifics of creating a career vision board, it's important to understand the distinction between a personal vision board and a career vision board. While vision boards have traditionally been associated with personal growth and development, they have also had significant impact as career planning and professional growth tools.

A traditional vision board often blends personal and professional aspirations. However, in this workbook, we focus specifically on a Career Vision Board, a targeted tool designed to map out your professional aspirations, skills, and goals. While a personal vision board may include relationships, health, or hobbies, a career vision board centers on job roles, industry growth, skills development, and leadership aspirations. What is the difference between these two vision boards, and why can't we combine them, *especially* since we do put general aspects of both categories together when we think of our goals? You can! But in this workbook, we want you to be more intentional about visualizing your career to then translate your vision into goals. At a glance, the scope, the content, and the purpose between a personal and career vision board are quite different. Therefore, we acknowledge that while both are powerful tools, they serve very *distinct* purposes and for the purposes of the following sections, are separated since we are focused on your professional career growth.

So, what is the difference?

A **personal** vision board encompasses various aspects of our lives including goals for personal growth, relationships, health, wellness, and hobbies. It usually reflects the aspects we would like to incorporate in our lives that will give us a sense of fulfillment on a personal level as we address a broad spectrum of those life goals and desired experiences. Personal goals are foundational to our career and success and as we continue this discussion we will begin to see and understand the important ties between our personal vision and career vision.

A **career** vision board is specific and centers around our professional aspirations, professional goals, and professional ambitions. It usually reflects elements on the path to the career and professional achievements we envision for ourselves. The process becomes more targeted and strategic, guiding us towards our professional objectives. From our "dream job" to professional development, it can reflect job titles, future career achievements, or even skills we hope to build as part of our career goals. By anchoring our career goals visually, we create a constant source of inspiration and focus that keeps us motivated and aligned on our path toward success. By creating a career-specific vision board, we ensure that our energy and actions are directed toward achieving our professional goals with precision and purpose.

In both instances, we can use those visualized aspirations and goals to help create actionable items including milestones, planned achievements, and development needed to attain the desired career.

Now that we have defined a career vision board, it is time for us to create one. The next exercise may require some self-reflection, but it is all about you, which means you are only bound by your imagination!

Reflecting on Your Career Aspirations

Let's get started! Take a moment to think about your career aspirations. What are they? What are your career visions for the future? As you think of your answers, flip back to Chapter 1 where you explored aspirations, passions and values.

Remember, aspirations are future-focused and do not have to be very specific. No pressure!

Our aspirations drive our goals which means our goals are the vehicle and how we can act behind those aspirations. Goals are action-oriented and are the steps we take to realize our vision. They tend to be nearer as we plan how accomplish but we will discuss goals in more detail in future sections.

Aspirations are what you represent on your vision board. To help us think more about our future aspirations, reflect on the questions below.

Describe your ideal career or dream job. What job roles or titles excite you? Consider job roles or titles that align with your passions and skills from Chapter 1. Some example job titles to inspire you include Entrepreneur, Consultant, Creative Director, Educator, Author, or Innovation Strategist. Feel free to mix and match elements to craft a career vision that suits you best!

_____

_____

_____

_____

_____

How will your ideal job make you feel? Think about the ideal work environment, what energizes you and brings out your best self.

_____

_____

_____

_____

_____

If you could have any future career achievements, what would they be?

_____

_____

_____

_____

_____

What skills do you wish to acquire or develop?

_____

_____

_____

_____

_____

How do you see your career evolving over the next 5, 10, or 20 years?

_____

_____

_____

_____

_____

How do you see the intersection of your values and career? How do your personal values influence your career choices?

_____

_____

_____

_____

What does professional success mean to you?

_____

_____

_____

_____

_____

Crafting Your Board

Now that you have reflected on our previous responses, it is time to visualize. Visuals allow for a better reflection of personal and professional experiences that individuals express through the art of presentation [4]. Visuals give a holistic view, allowing us to observe the interconnections between our aspirations and how they may depend on each other.

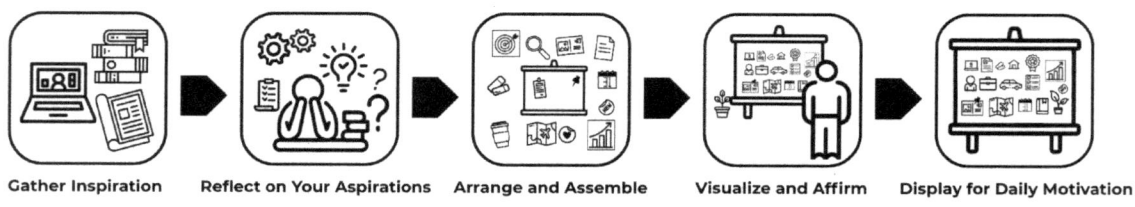

Gather Inspiration   Reflect on Your Aspirations   Arrange and Assemble   Visualize and Affirm   Display for Daily Motivation

Step 1: Gather Inspiration

Before you start cutting and pasting, take a moment to explore your inner vision. Think about your biggest career dreams—the job titles, industries, and achievements to which you aspire. Then, gather materials that bring these ideas to life:

- Magazines with career-relevant images

- Digital inspiration from Pinterest, LinkedIn, or Google images
- Powerful quotes that fuel your ambition
- Icons, logos, or symbols representing your dream companies or industries

Write down five words that define your career vision in Appendix A before moving to Step 2. This step is not about perfection. It's about collecting elements that ignite a sense of purpose and excitement.

Step 2: Reflect on Your Aspirations

Reflect on the answers to the prompt questions you answered previously in this chapter. Consider how each of your answers aligns with the visual elements you have selected. Do the images, words, or even quotes you have selected encapsulate your career goals and aspirations? For example, ask yourself:

- Does this image or word reflect my professional ambitions?
- How does this align with my vision for the next 5, 10, or 20 years?
- Does this inspire action or reinforce my belief in achieving my goals?

Step 3: Arrange and Assemble

Use the box in Appendix A to place your choice elements. This is an opportunity to arrange them in a way that feels meaningful (e.g. thematically, chronologically etc.), customizing your vision board in a way that feels intuitive and inspiring for you where you can reflect on it and hold yourself accountable. This is meant to be a "mini" vision board to get you started on the career vision board process, but you are encouraged to create a representation - whether it be as big as a canvas or small as a letter sized sheet - that can be hung or placed in a space where you can view it daily.

Step 4: Visualize and Affirm

It's time to visualize and affirm now that your vision board is complete. Take the time to not just visualize but internalize as you "see" yourself achieving the career goals you have laid out.

Don't be afraid to read out loud the words and quotes you have added to further reinforce the manifestation of your aspirations as you visualize. Your vision board is more than a collection of images; it's a living representation of your career journey.

Step 5: Display for Daily Motivation

The final step is all about you placing your vision board in a place where you can regularly see it to reflect on your career goals and your progress towards achieving them. Remember, vision boards are not one and done. It is important to revisit what you have created to stay motivated, and laser-focused on your professional path. By visually representing our aspirations, we tap into the subconscious mind, reinforcing our intentions and keeping them at the forefront of our consciousness. A career vision board can be used as a visual roadmap to translate career goals into actions and tasks that are necessary to stay on the career trajectory outlined. By actively engaging with your vision board, you transform it from a static display into a powerful catalyst.

Using Your Vision Board

This process should be a transformative experience as you apply the lessons from Chapter 1, to help you clarify your career aspirations into a visual representation. In the next chapter, we will leverage the vision board as we take the key themes, goals, and aspirations and create an inspirational statement that articulate career aspirations concisely. This statement will encapsulate your goals and values, serving as a guiding light as you navigate your career.

Remember, your vision board is a starting point—a launchpad for dreams and a roadmap to success. Take this creative process seriously, and it will become one of your most powerful career development tools.

CHAPTER 3

Creating a Career Vision Statement

"Create the highest, grandest vision possible for your life because you become what you believe."
—Oprah Winfrey

Remember the story from the Introduction of the sailor who didn't have a map? Let's revisit the story. While the sailor may have seen many interesting things along the way, because he didn't have a map to his destination and without direction, he likely ended up farther from where he wanted to be. This what a career journey can feel like without a clear vision: lots of activity and even some interesting experiences along the way but no meaningful direction. To find direction, you need a compass. The career vision statement can serve as your compass. Therefore, before we begin the process of translating our vision into an action plan that can help us achieve our career goals, we must first create a vision statement.

Career Vision

Career vision represents a picture of the future career path you would like to pursue informed by your personal values, brand, and professional goals, serving as a guiding beacon or "north star" for career growth. The aligned career vision is a result of your values and what you believe intersecting with your brand and who you are, driving career goals and trajectory. Leveraging each of these, you can formulate a career vision. We can derive a career vision statement by using the career vision. But first, we need to understand the differences between the Career Vision and the Career Vision Statement.

While the terms "career vision" and "career vision statement" are closely related, they serve distinct purposes and play unique roles in shaping your professional journey.

Think of your **career vision** as the **big picture** of what you want your professional life to look like in the future. It's a high-level view of your long-term goals and aspirations. It encompasses where you see yourself, the type of work you want to do, the impact you want to have, and how your career aligns with your personal values and passions. The career vision acts as a "north star" guiding and helping to align your choices and actions. It helps you answer the "why" questions behind your career ambitions.

Table 3: Elements of Vision

Elements	The Definition of Elements
Personal Brand	Think of your personal brand as the intersection between your skills, including your unique strengths, and personality. That intersection is people's perception of you and how they see you.
Career Desire	The specific aspirations and milestones you want to achieve, like the roles you aim for, the industries you are passionate about, or the impact you want to make.
Values	Your individual beliefs that guide you and motivate you and your behavior.

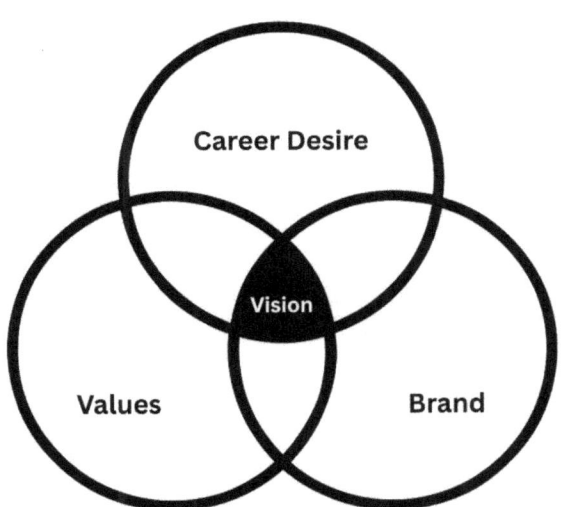

Your career vision is the picture of your desired future state in your professional journey. It emerges from the holistic view of your values, personal brand, and career desires, forming the intersection where your true professional purpose lies.

The foundation of your career vision statement lies in the intersection of four key elements: **Vision**, **Values**, **Personal Brand**, and **Career Desire**. The resulting vision statement becomes your **North Star**, in written form.

In contrast, the **career vision statement** is a **concise, actionable statement** that captures the essence of your career vision. It transforms the big-picture ideas of your career vision into a focused guiding statement that is actionable and clearly defines your professional purpose and long-term goals.

How They Work Together

- **The Career Vision** is your **dream,** the larger narrative of your professional life and aspirations. It's expansive, flexible, and deeply personal, offering a holistic view of your career aspirations.
- **The Career Vision Statement** is your **guide**, a focused, practical articulation of your career vision. It's a tool that helps you communicate and implement your vision in a way that aligns your goals and actions with your aspirations.

Career Vision Statement

Companies often use vision statements to communicate and guide employees toward one shared goal. The vision statement is meant as a motivation to provide purpose and inspiration with the hopes of improving employee efficiency. Company vision statements are important because they provide direction and primary long-term goals for the business. A vision can also be viewed as a leader's statement that emphasizes a desired, long-term future state for an organization. Vision statements are powerful because they articulate a future state—something worth striving for.

When we read more on the definition of a company's vision statement, we see keywords such as guide, goal, long-term, and desire. Similarly, our career vision statement provides a direction for our professional life. It's not just about *what* we want to achieve but *why* it matters. It encapsulates long-term goals and the values that guide us, allowing us to make career choices that align with our authentic selves.

We define our career vision statement as a formal statement that reflects and describes what we want to achieve in the future and the impact we would like to have through our professional goals. Our vision statement defines what we as individuals want as long-term goals and is an expression of our desired state within our career. Think of it as the answer to the question: **"What do I want to be when I grow up?"** But with a richer, deeper understanding of who we are today and where we aspire to be tomorrow. It points us in the right direction for decision-making and goal setting. Your career vision statement is meant to inspire and energize. It provides clarity on what you would like your career to look like for the future.

By creating a career vision statement, you can transform your aspirations into a clear and actionable guide that informs your choices, motivates you, and keeps you aligned with your long-term ambitions. Whether you are just starting out, transitioning to a new role, or aiming for the pinnacle of your profession, your career vision statement is a source of inspiration and direction that reminds you why you do what you do.

Leveraging Your Vision Board

Before we begin crafting a career vision statement, there are a few questions we need to answer. But first, let's revisit the career vision board you created in the previous chapter. Your vision board was a creative and visual exercise to help you define your career aspirations. It contains symbols, images, quotes, and themes that represent what you want from your career.

Take a moment to reflect on your career vision board:

- What themes or goals stand out?
- What values are depicted visually?
- What kind of work environments, roles, or achievements are represented?

These are the building blocks of your career vision statement. By leveraging your career vision board to create a career vision statement, you can articulate your long-term career aspirations more clearly and effectively, guiding your career decisions and actions in alignment with your goals and values.

Because career vision boards are visual representations of professional aspirations, goals, and ambitions, you can now extract the key themes, goals and aspirations represented on the board. When reviewing your vision board, ask yourself, what are the overarching aspirations that you have depicted? Once you have answered that question, it is time to think about the core values (remember the values you wrote down in Chapter 1?) that drive and motivate you. Like the alignment to our career vision, our values are also foundational to the formulated vision. Our values are the standards and principles we believe and live by, which means that as we navigate our career, there will also be moments that we reflect on if career decisions and opportunities align with who we are and our beliefs. Keeping in mind what we have reviewed, let's take a few steps to craft a career vision statement.

Steps on Crafting a Career Vision Statement

Crafting a career vision statement is a reflective and creative process. The steps below allow you to build a statement that reflects your core beliefs, builds on your personal brand, and encompasses your career aspirations. These are all elements of from Chapter 1. Review what you wrote in those earlier exercises and bring them forward here to help with your vision statement. It may seem a bit repetitive but trust the process.

Step 1: Reflect on Your Values

Your vision statement should be rooted in these values so that it aligns with who you are and what you believe.

What principles guide you personally and professionally? What are your beliefs? What kind of impact do you want to have?

_____

_____

_____

_____

_____

_____

Step 2: Your Personal Brand Statement

Your "Personal Brand," a term we hear quite often, refers to how others perceive you professionally. this statement should reflect your strengths, skills, and the qualities that make you unique.

What are you known for? What do you want to be known for in the future? What skills or attributes do you want others to recognize in you?

_____

_____

_____

_____

_____

_____

Step 3: Summarize Your Career Aspirations

Based on key themes and insights from your reflections on your aspirations (Chapter 1), summarize your long-term aspirations in a few key points. Reflect on what you imagine for your career. Think about the impact you want to have, goals and milestones you want to achieve.

What kind of career do you envision for yourself? What roles or achievements do you aspire to? What kind of legacy do you want to leave in your field?

_____

_____

_____

_____

_____

_____

_____

Step 4: Craft your Statement

Using the answers from the previous steps and the information you have gathered from the previous chapters, it's time to craft your career vision statement. The statement should be in concise, clear, and motivating. It should also be inspiring, and forward-looking, encompassing your professional purpose and the impact you aspire to make in your chosen field. Here is a simple formula you can follow to get you started. This shouldn't be your final version but rather a starting point as you continue to revise your career vision statement. An example template is provided in Appendix B.

"To [insert a specific goal you want to achieve – desired end state] by [insert how you would like to contribute to the field or make an impact] in [specific field or role], guided by [values or personal brand]."

"To establish myself as a [desired professional title] recognized for [key skill or expertise] within the [industry], utilizing my passion for [specific area of interest] to [positive impact you want to make] and consistently deliver innovative solutions that [desired outcome for clients or stakeholders]."

_____

_____

_____

_____

_____

_____

_____

_____

Step 5: Refine and Iterate

Crafting the right vision statement that accurately reflects your career aspirations takes refinement and tweaking. Take time to iterate, asking trusted mentors and peers for feedback. Ask them if it is clear, and if they understand what you want to achieve in the future, and the impact, based on what they have read. What are some of the comments that can help you improve and strengthen your statement?

Does it resonate with who you are? Does it clearly capture your ambitions? Is it inspiring?

Use feedback to refine your statement until it truly reflects your career aspirations.

_____

_____

_____

_____

_____

_____

Step 6: Finalize and Display Your Career Vision Statement

While your career vision statement will evolve throughout your career, at this point it is important to settle on a vision statement. Once you are satisfied, write the final career vision statement below and then transfer it to a place where you can see it often as it serves as inspiration and guidance. Put it on your desk, your vision board, or even as a daily reminder on your phone.

_____

_____

_____

_____

_____

_____

In this chapter, we explored how to create a career vision statement by reflecting on your values, personal brand, and aspirations. We also outlined how we can leverage our vision board to extract key themes to help us craft our career vision statement. As we think about the role our values, personal brand, and career aspirations play, we reflect on how each of these is defined and how it contributes to our career vision statement. The vision statement can serve as motivation and guidance on a path towards long-term professional goals. It enables us to stay aligned to our aspirations and can be used as a motivation, while being leveraged to help us articulate aspirations into career objectives which in turn can help us develop actionable goals. When we align our career vision statements, objectives and goals, these help us down a path of intentionality and purpose for our career. But remember, our vision statement is not static—it will evolve as you grow, just as your goals and dreams will change over time. Let it guide you, motivate you, and remind you of the impact you want to make.

In the next chapter, we'll take your vision statement and translate it into concrete career objectives, turning your aspirations into actionable milestones. Let's keep building your path to a fulfilling professional journey.

CHAPTER 4

Drafting Vision Goals

"Your vision becomes your blueprint,
and your actions become the building blocks."
—Anonymous

As we follow our roadmap, we see that we have gone from reflecting on our aspirations, to making physical representations with our career vision board, then distilling that vision board down to our career vision statement. We continue to add details with each step, focusing this chapter on draft goals based on our vision. Our career vision statement serves as the foundation for drafting meaningful and strategic vision goals. While our vision statement answers the question of "What do I want to become?", this chapter is focused on setting a strategy through our goals and answering the question, "What do I need to do to accomplish my vision?".

In Chapter 3, our career vision statement is the compass we need to ensure we are pointed in the right direction. Now that we have direction, we need clear markers and steps along the way to ensure we are charting the course, headed in the right direction. Drafting goals is a critical step after creating the vision statement as it serves as a foundation for more detailed and specific planning later.

As we actively use our career vision statement as a guide for career decisions, we now need to take that guidance and break it down into high-level long-term goals. These will further be used to define objectives which will eventually lead to daily activities and actions that should align to the high-level goals. We use these goals and objectives to get to the destination of our ultimate vision.

It is important to note that goals tend to be more high-level and strategic, defining an overall direction, compared to objectives, which can be tactical, defining specific actions. Below, we highlight some differences between goals and objectives.

Goals vs. Objectives

The difference between goals and objectives lies in their scope, focus, and purpose. Goals tend to be broad and general with long-term outcomes you aim to accomplish. Goals provide direction and can help define your career vision. In contrast, objectives are specific and actionable steps that help us achieve a goal. Objectives tend to define the "how" to achieve a goal and help to break goals down into manageable parts that can be achieved over a short term. Your goals set the direction based on your vision and your objectives form the map that will get you there.

Here is a framework way to remember the differences between Goals and Objectives:

Table 4: F.A.S.T. Framework

	Goals	**Objectives**
Focus	Focus on the big picture	Focus on specific actions
Ambition	Ambitious and aspirational	Achievable and measurable
Scope	Broad	Narrow
Timeframe	Long-term (3-5 years)	Short-term (6-18 months)

Goal: Successfully Launch My Book *Visualize Your Professional Future* in 2025

Objectives:

1. Complete manuscript and finalize content by March 2025.
2. Secure publishing and distribution strategy through hybrid publishing services to align to publishing date of Q3 2025.
3. Develop a marketing and promotion plan for social media and potential partnerships.

The example shows that while the goal is defined at a high level focusing on the bigger picture and encapsulating aspirations on a long-term timeline, the objectives are more action oriented with narrower scope on a shorter timeline. We will explore objectives more in the following chapter.

From Vision to Goals

Use the following steps to help you analyze your career vision statement for goal drafting.

Step 1: Review Your Career Vision Statement

Restate the career vision statement you drafted in the previous chapter:

_____

_____

_____

_____

Step 2: Identify the core themes or components within your vision statement.

To go from our career vision statement to our vision goals, we need to identify the major components of the statement above. Drafting our goals requires us to think strategically, but what does that mean? It means we need to be intentional as we analyze the factors and variables that can influence our long-term career success that we have stated within the vision statement. It involves seeing the big picture and planning ahead, which then allows us to put thought into action.

What are the key components? *(Examples: leadership development, business acumen, global outreach)*

_____

_____

_____

_____

Step 3: Drafting Vision Goals

Using the components identified, create three to four high-level goals that can collectively fulfill your career vision statement. First, here is an example of a career vision statement and a few suggested goals.

"To become a respected technology leader who bridges business and technical teams while mentoring the next generation of tech performers."

Example Vision Goals:
Goal #1: Develop executive level business acumen
Goal #2: Build a track record of successful cross-functional projects
Goal #3: Establish a formal mentorship program

Before you set out to draft your goals, it's important to keep in mind some of the common challenges to overcome should you encounter them. Firstly, though goals are meant to be broad in scope, they shouldn't be so broad that they end up being vague and not measurable. Secondly, vision goals must always bridge to the career vision; sometimes drafted goals may lack career vision alignment. Lastly, yes, a career vision statement is important, and you may feel compelled to set several goals. However, if we set too many goals then we end up losing focus, hampering the path to achieving the career vision statement.

Now it's time to give drafting your goals a try using your career vision statement from Step 1.

My Vision Goals:

Goal #1:

Goal #2:

Goal #3:

Goal #4:

Step 4: Test Your Goals and Ensure Alignment

Now that you have drafted your career vision goals it is time to review them in detail. This ensures that they are clearly defined to help you fulfill your career vision statement and that you are aligned with your values, brand, and career aspirations. Use this checklist to test your goals and refine them as necessary.

- Does this goal contribute to the big picture of my career vision?
- Is this goal achievable within 3-5 years?
- Have I ensured this goal challenges and excites me?
- Does this goal align with my core values and priorities?

Refining My Vision Goals:

Goal #1:

Goal #2:

Goal #3:

Goal #4:

The Bridge to Objectives

You have taken a very important step of drafting high-level vision goals that align to your career aspirations. Drafting career vision goals is not straightforward and as your career vision statement evolves, your goals will evolve. Refinement is part of the process but drafting these goals is the first step toward turning your aspirations into a reality. These goals are key to your career roadmap, providing clarity and focus. While these goals can be powerful and serve an important purpose, they are still broad and conceptual. The next step is to transform them so that they are specific, actionable, and measurable. Think of your career vision goals as the milestones on your map, key destinations that mark your progress along the way. Objectives, on the other hand, are the paths you will follow to reach each milestone. Together, they create a comprehensive strategy for achieving your career vision.

In the next chapter, we will further refine these goals by breaking them into well-defined and actionable objectives. These objectives will be the tactical steps necessary to move closer to realizing your career vision. Through measurable benchmarks and realistic timeframes, your objectives will provide a guide to your progress.

CHAPTER 5

Turning Vision into Action

"A Goal is just a daydream,
unless there is a plan and active steps to achieve it."
—Dr. Malika Grayson-Duncan

In the last chapter, we identified high-level goals from our career vision statement which serve as milestones guiding us forward. But, how do we know we have hit a milestone on the way to our goal? What are the measurable steps? Objectives serve as those actionable and measurable steps that help us achieve those goals. Remember, goals give us the direction, and the milestones help us know we are headed in that right direction, while the objectives ensure we put one foot in front of the other and move forward.

Do you recall the differences between goals and objectives? We need to understand the clear distinction as we begin to further refine and distill our goals into objectives.

Remember: Goals are **broad, strategic, high-level, and long-term — aligned to the career vision statement.**

Objectives are **specific, tactical, detailed and short-term — aligned to the goals.**

With our high-level goals defined, the next step is to translate them into actionable objectives using the SMART Framework, a proven method for measuring progress. From performance objectives to health objectives [5-6], the SMART Framework is a well-established model that has been employed across numerous industries to measure impact and provide structure towards achieving goals. It is also a great 'temperature check' to determine if the goals that have been set are clearly defined.

The SMART Framework Defined

Let's use an example to review the SMART Framework:

Goal: "Gain functional management and people leadership experience to prepare for higher leadership roles."

Table 5: SMART Framework Example

Component	Meaning	In Practice
Specific	Objectives should be specific and clearly defined Question to Ask: What exactly do you want to accomplish?	"Take a course on emotional intelligence to enhance my skills as a manager"
Measurable	Objectives should include criteria to track progress Questions to Ask: What is the metric you will use to track progress? How will you know when the objective has been achieved?	"Take 3 leadership courses for new managers within six months of new management position"
Achievable	Objectives should be feasible and attainable Questions to Ask: Are the objectives within reach? Do you have the resources and bandwidth?	"With the 16 hours allotted I have for training, I can take 2 courses"
Relevant	Objectives should align with your vision and goals Questions to Ask: Do the objectives contribute to your long-term aspirations? Are the objectives relevant to the goal?	"I need some leadership courses to support my goal of becoming a people leader"
Time-bound	Objectives should have a timeframe for completion Questions to Ask: When will this objective be accomplished? What is the timeline?	"Complete leadership training courses and certifications by (a specific time period – e.g. within six months)"

As we start with our career vision goals and begin the step-by-step process of breaking down those goals into objectives, there are a few questions to ask:

1. **What are the key focus areas for my goal?**

    Goal: "Develop functional management and people leadership experience to prepare for higher leadership roles." Key focus area for this goal may be (i) Team Management and Development, (ii) Performance Reviews and Feedback (iii) Cross-Functional Collaboration (iv) Communication Skills

    _____

    _____

    _____

    _____

    _____

2. **What actions are required to meet this goal?**

    This is where we can define our actions by using a SMART Objectives template to list the actions or objectives to help us achieve our goal.

    _____

    _____

    _____

    _____

    _____

3. **Who are the individuals in the supporting roles that can provide help to meet this goal?**

Depending on your goal, you may be able to leverage a point of contact within your network. This requires you to do an audit of your network so that you can evaluate your network and your interconnections. This will help you understand how the people in your network can help to achieve those goals. Use the career network map template in the Appendix C as a starting point.

_____

_____

_____

_____

_____

_____

_____

4. **How should these objectives be prioritized?**

Objectives should be ranked based on urgency, impact, or feasibility as they relate to the goal.

_____

_____

_____

_____

_____

_____

_____

5. **What are the barriers to achieving this objective and what are the limitations? How do we overcome them?**

Understanding the constraints of our objectives and brainstorming the strategies to navigate will allow for adaptation and refinement as challenges arise.

_____

_____

_____

_____

_____

_____

_____

Drafting Objectives

Using your goals from Chapter 4, follow the process for breaking down goals into objectives. Try listing your objectives in priority order. This will help ensure there is focus on the most critical objectives as you create a logical sequence where some objectives may need to build off others to achieve the aligned goal, especially goals that require a step-by-step approach. Prioritizing will also help you better manage the available resources, especially if there is a limitation thus allowing you to allocate efficiently.

GOAL #1

	Objectives (SMART)	Start Date	End Date	Support	Success Metric
1.					
2.					
3.					
4.					

GOAL #2

	Objectives (SMART)	Start Date	End Date	Support	Success Metric
1.					
2.					
3.					
4.					

GOAL #3

	Objectives (SMART)	Start Date	End Date	Support	Success Metric
1.					
2.					
3.					
4.					

GOAL #4

	Objectives (SMART)	Start Date	End Date	Support	Success Metric
1.					
2.					
3.					
4.					

Implementing Objectives

We started with our aspirations and have continued to restate at each level using the activities in this workbook. From our vision goals we were able to define our SMART objectives – now we take it one step further. With our goals and objectives defined, the next steps in our workbook roadmap focuses on implementation. Implementation refers to the process of executing a plan, strategy, or design to achieve a specific goal or outcome. It requires taking action and having a structured approach to arrive at a tangible result. In this section, we will discuss the actions needed for effective implementation of our objectives.

What tasks and activities are required or need to be completed to accomplish our objectives? Implementation isn't just about a task list but requires strategic planning to ensure effective execution. Part of that planning includes ongoing tracking to ensure that progress is being made towards the milestones with any necessary adjustments.

Developing an Action Plan

To begin the implementation process, let's break down one of your SMART objectives using the following template. The result gives us a detailed action plan that gives an outline of the tasks required for implementation.

Restate one of your objectives:

_____

_____

_____

What specific actions or tasks must be completed to achieve the objective?

_____

_____

_____

What resources are needed to support the completion of the tasks outlined above? Resources can range from financial resources to individuals to tools. Do you have access to all the resources you need? If not, a task may be required as part of your action plan to gain access to the necessary resources.

_____

_____

_____

The table below is a high-level representation of the implementation process. Appendix C provides a template to help you further refine your action plan.

SMART Objectives	Actionable Steps	Resources Need	Due Date	Success Metric
1. **Objective 1**	a. Task 1 b. Task 2 c. Task 3			
2. **Objective 2**	a. Task 1 b. Task 2 c. Task 3			
3. **Objective 3**	a. Task 1 b. Task 2 c. Task 3			

While developing an action plan plays an important role in understanding the tasks required to achieve objectives, it is equally important to establish accountability to make certain progress is tracked and deadlines are met. Included in your action plan should also be cadence—are you going to track progress weekly, monthly, quarterly? The answer depends on the specific task as some tasks may not require as much rigor as others when it comes to monitoring. Regular check-ins, whether weekly, bi-weekly, or monthly, create structured opportunities for self-reflection and course correction, ensuring that momentum is maintained even when challenges arise.

Regular tracking can also help with anticipating and ultimately adapting whenever there are challenges. As you think about the action plan for each objective, also spend time to reflect on the potential obstacles or challenges that may be encountered while executing the action plan.

Continue to brainstorm potential challenges, taking the opportunity to also develop strategies to help solve them. Keep in mind, this is just an anticipation of what may happen and isn't necessarily a prediction. Therefore, be flexible and willing to adjust course, if necessary, to stay on track with tasks as you move towards your goals.

SMART Objectives	Actionable Steps	Potential Challenges	Potential Solutions
Objective:	Task:		
	Task:		
	Task:		
Objective:	Task:		
	Task:		
	Task:		

SMART Objectives	Actionable Steps	Potential Challenges	Potential Solutions
Objective:	Task:		
	Task:		
	Task:		

Achieving your career vision goals requires more than just setting objectives and developing an action plan, it demands discipline, consistency, and sustained motivation. While a well thought-out and structured action plan provides direction, accountability and motivation serve as the driving forces that keep everything on track. Strong accountability mechanisms are essential to ensuring there is follow-through on tasks. One of the most effective ways to do this is by engaging an accountability partner. This is someone who can provide guidance, check in on progress, and hold you responsible for the steps you have committed to taking. This could be a mentor, a peer, a coach, or even a family member who you have shared your plans with. Studies have found that individuals who recorded their goals, shared them with a friend, and provided weekly updates were significantly more likely to achieve their goals, showing the positive impact of accountability on goal attainment. [7]

Because tracking progress requires frequent check-ins, a tracking tool can be useful and an integral part of accomplishing goals. In addition to having an accountability partner, tracking tools can play a vital role in maintaining progress. There are several tools available for tracking and more become available each day. It's recommended to try a few of the tools to find the one that works best for you and your tracking goals. Goal-tracking apps, digital planners, or even simple spreadsheets allow for easy documentation of milestones, adjustments, and lessons learned along the way. Using a tool can help you better track your SMART objectives, especially across a timeframe and the action plans that detail them, while allowing for the flexibility needed to adapt or make changes.

Beyond accountability, staying motivated is crucial in bringing career aspirations to life. Motivation naturally fluctuates, so having strategies to sustain enthusiasm is key. Revisiting your vision board that you have created from the earlier chapters can be a powerful motivator. Spending just a few minutes daily reflecting on your future success can help reaffirm your purpose. As you reflect, think about what you have already accomplished and reward those wins. Remember, this is a journey and is a sustained effort that will have both wins and obstacles.

Bringing Your Vision to Life

In this chapter we focused turning broad career vision goals into a detailed plan needed to successfully achieve our career vision goals. Using this approach, we have created several paths that form a cohesive roadmap for achieving our long-term aspirations.

We began by exploring the importance of turning broad career vision goals into more actionable, measurable steps. By defining the high-level career vision goals and breaking them down into SMART objectives, we have created a structured pathway toward achieving our aspirations. However, setting objectives is just the first step, implementation is where the real transformation happens and why a development plan is necessary to ensure we are intentional on the path.

Executing the tasks required to achieve our objectives and ultimately make our career vision a reality requires consistency, accountability, and adaptability. The action plan is a living document that should evolve as progress is made and new opportunities or challenges are encountered. Rounding off task execution with strong accountability and motivation strategies is crucial.

Remember, the difference between an aspiration and a goal is action, and this chapter provides a template for you to translate those aspirations into action.

CHAPTER 6

Bringing It All Together

"The whole is greater than the sum of its parts."
—Aristotle

Now, let's synthesize everything from the first five chapters, connecting your vision, goals, and the concrete steps to make them a reality. Up to this point, you have reflected on your aspirations, identified your strengths, and outlined impactful moments that have shaped your path. You have set SMART objectives, built a structured plan, and learned strategies for overcoming challenges. Embrace the vision you have crafted, take bold action, and build the future you deserve.

Revisiting Chapter 1: Envisioning Your Future – A Journey of Self-Discovery

In Chapter 1, we began with self-discovery, exploring how aspirations serve as the compass guiding us toward our most authentic potential. Vision doesn't happen by accident; it requires deep reflection, honest self-assessment, and a commitment to personal growth.

We examined the power of aspirations and their role in shaping our path. Aspirations help us:

- Navigate complex career decisions.
- Maintain resilience in the face of adversity.
- Align actions with our authentic selves.
- Make meaningful progress toward significant goals.

Through structured exercises, we identified core desires, strengths, and values that influence our career vision. We also explored the Five Tenets of Transformation, a framework designed to help us create with intention, imagine audaciously, believe unwaveringly, synthesize insights for transformation, and break through limitations.

Revisiting Chapter 2: Creating a Career Vision Board

In Chapter 2, we introduced the power of visualization as a tool to bring aspirations to life. Scientific research shows that mental imagery activates neural pathways that improve motivation, focus, and goal attainment. We explored how career vision boards serve as tangible representations of professional aspirations, reinforcing clarity and motivation in the journey ahead.

We also discussed the difference between personal and career vision boards. While personal vision boards focus on life goals such as relationships, health, and well-being, career vision boards center around professional aspirations, skills, and achievements. By crafting a targeted career vision board, we created a strategic tool to guide career decisions and professional development.

Revisiting Chapter 3: Creating a Career Vision Statement

In Chapter 3, we built upon our career vision board by crafting a career vision statement—a powerful compass to ensure we stay on course. Like the sailor lost at sea, we emphasize the risks of drifting aimlessly.

We explored how a career vision represents a big-picture view of our professional aspirations, shaped by our values, personal brand, and career desires. To refine this vision, we developed a career vision statement, which serves as a guiding beacon to align decisions and actions with long-term aspirations.

With our vision statement in place, the next logical step was defining high-level goals in Chapter 4.

Revisiting Chapter 4: Drafting Vision Goals

In Chapter 4, we took our career vision statement and transformed it into structured high-level career goals. While our vision statement answered the "why," our goals answered the "what". What do we need to do to accomplish our vision?

We also established the difference between goals and objectives:

- Goals provide broad, long-term direction based on our vision.

- Objectives are tactical, short-term, and measurable steps that drive us toward achieving those goals.

By setting strategic goals, we created a roadmap that would later be broken down into SMART objectives in the next chapter.

Revisiting Chapter 5: Turning Vision into Action

In Chapter 5, we transitioned from setting goals to defining actionable, measurable steps to drive progress. We introduced the SMART framework, ensuring that objectives were:

- Specific – Clearly defined and focused
- Measurable – Able to track progress and success
- Achievable – Realistic and attainable
- Relevant – Aligned with long-term career aspirations
- Time-bound – With defined deadlines for accountability

By breaking down goals into SMART objectives, we moved from aspiration to execution, ensuring that our goals weren't just ideas but concrete steps leading to measurable progress.

This chapter also introduced accountability and motivation strategies, emphasizing the role of mentors, coaches, and accountability partners in keeping us on track. We explored ways to stay motivated such as tracking progress using tools or career planners and celebrating small wins to sustain momentum.

Execution: The Key to Lasting Success

Now that we have built a structured roadmap, the next step is execution. Your development plan is a living, evolving document that will change as you grow, face new challenges, and uncover new opportunities.

To ensure continued progress:

- Commit to continuous learning. Be open to acquiring new skills and adjusting your goals as needed.
- Leverage your support system. Check in with mentors, accountability partners, and peers to maintain motivation.
- Measure your progress. Use tracking tools and regularly reassess milestones.
- Recognize achievements, both big and small as motivation.

Moving Forward with Confidence

Bringing your vision to life isn't about waiting for the perfect moment, it's about taking intentional, consistent action. You now have a structured approach to defining and executing your career aspirations, a set of tools to keep you accountable, and a mindset built for success.

As you move forward, remember: Your future isn't something you wait for, it's something you create. Every decision, every step forward, and every moment of resilience brings you closer to the extraordinary career and life you envision.

This is your moment. Take the first step, then keep going.

CHAPTER 7

Sustaining Momentum

"Success is not final; failure is not fatal;
it is the courage to continue that counts."
—Winston Churchill

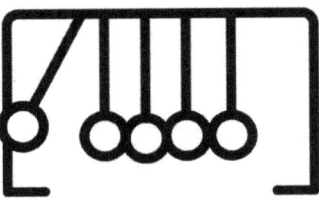

Your career journey will not be linear, just like the sailing a boat. A sailor must constantly adjust to the elements, geography and various factors within and without their control. No matter how amazing your vision or how detailed your plan, unexpected challenges, disruptions, pivots, and opportunities will arise. The key to long-term success is not just in planning but in adapting, evolving, and sustaining momentum through transformation. You must learn how to thrive in disruption and at times reinvent yourself.

Throughout this book you have done the hard work to define your career vision, set strategic goals, develop an action plan, and establish accountability measures. Congratulations!

Now the focus shifts to ensuring your vision remains relevant as industries evolve, new opportunities emerge, and your own aspirations shift. The last pages will guide you through sustaining motivation, adapting to change, managing career transitions, and building resilience so your career vision continues to guide you professionally.

Staying Motivated Through Challenges

The initial excitement of crafting a vision and setting goals is energizing. However, as time passes, daily responsibilities, setbacks, and competing priorities can cause you to second guess your strategy and approach. The key to remaining focused and motivated is consistent engagement and intentional reinforcement of your goals. Regular reflection and goal reassessment are essential practices to continue to embrace a growth mindset and an evolving approach to your career. Here are a few recommendations:

- Scheduling monthly, quarterly, or biannual check-ins with mentors, accountability partners, and coaches helps track progress, address challenges, and refine goals.
- Asking yourself, and these key stakeholders, whether your goals still align with your vision, while considering changes or new opportunities that could impact your professional trajectory.
- Keeping a career journal as a tracking tool to document key insights and track progress provides perspective on how far you have come. Celebrating small wins,

whether it's completing a course, building a new skill, or expanding your network, helps sustain your motivation and engagement.

- Leveraging your support system and career sponsors offers an opportunity for guidance and encouragement.
- Engaging with professional communities that align with your career goals can also provide inspiration and valuable learning opportunities.

Adapting and Expanding Your Vision

Your career vision will change as you gain experience, learn new skills, and discover new opportunities. What seemed like a perfect career path five years ago may no longer align with your values or aspirations today. As factors change, it is important that you be intentional about recognizing when your career vision needs to be adjusted. If you feel unfulfilled despite achieving your goals, it may be time for a shift or realignment. Stay informed about industry trends, getting ahead of shifting focus areas or new emerging technologies. This ensures that your vision remains relevant. Finally, adjusting your vision doesn't mean giving up on your original goals. It means evolving with intention. If a change in career direction is needed, incremental changes such as exploring new projects, learning new skills, or taking on expanded statement of work, can pave the way for a smoother transition or perhaps an exponential gain.

Managing Career Transitions with Confidence

Transitions require a strategic approach whether you are seeking a promotion, switching industries, or stepping into leadership. Proactive planning for career transitions ensures that you are prepared rather than forced into change. If you are aiming for a promotion, proactively developing key skills and expanding your network will give you an edge. If you are considering a career pivot, researching transferable skills and engaging in learning opportunities relevant to the new field can help you accelerate the transition.

Fear and self-doubt are natural in career transitions. The secret? Don't wait to feel ready. Take action anyway. Confidence isn't a prerequisite; it's the result of pushing through discomfort. Doubt can be reframed as an opportunity for growth, enabling you to take on challenges and become more resilient and capable.

Building Resilience and Handling Setbacks

Setbacks are inevitable. Whether it's a job loss, a missed promotion, or an industry shift, resilience is the key to rebounding stronger. Instead of viewing setbacks as failures, they should be seen as valuable feedback. Adapt the mindset of asking yourself what can be learned from any of these experiences and how they can be used for improvement. This shifts the perspective from failure to growth.

Developing a growth mindset is essential. A fixed mindset might say, "I'm not good at this," whereas a growth mindset reframes it as, "I'm not good at this yet, but I can develop the skills I need." The ability to adapt and persist determines long-term success.

Future-Proofing Your Career

As we have mentioned, the workplace is evolving rapidly, and staying relevant requires continuous learning and strategic positioning. Longevity requires staying ahead of change rather than reacting to it. This means continually increasing and improving your skills, staying up to date on emerging trends in your profession, industry, and role, ensuring that you understand the potential longevity of your career.

Continually growing and maintaining your network remains a key strategy for career resilience. Engaging with industry peers, joining professional organizations, and actively building relationships before you need them can open new doors which may lead to future career opportunities. Seeking sponsors (i.e., senior colleagues who advocate on your behalf to support your career growth and advancement) both within and outside of your organization or business can provide further career opportunities and insights. Additionally, committing to lifelong learning can help ensure career longevity.

Building a strong personal brand and thought leadership also play a vital role in career sustainability. Sharing insights, participating in industry discussions, and positioning yourself as a subject matter expert and thought leader can help expand your influence and improve your career and growth opportunities.

Success is an Ongoing Journey

Life happens, disruption happens, and failure happens. Things change and winds shift. At this point you have all the workbook principles and concepts. You are ready to apply them to create a lasting personal vision, vision statement and achievable goals. Your career vision will shape your professional life, but your personal choices will also impact your overall fulfillment. By finding the harmony between both aspects, you will be able to create a harmonious and exciting journey and be more strategic about designing a holistic life by intention, not by chance.

What are your next steps?

1. Stay focused, stay committed, and stay resilient.
2. Track your progress.
3. Leverage your network.
4. Embrace a growth mindset.
5. Proactively address obstacles.
6. Use the tools and ideas in this workbook.

Now, it's time to put your plan into motion. The actions you take today will shape your future success.

Your Career Vision Toolkit

This appendix contains a collection of worksheets, templates, and exercises designed to help you put the concepts from this book into action. Whether you are clarifying your career vision, setting strategic goals, or mapping out your next steps, these tools will guide you through the process in a structured and meaningful way.

Each exercise aligns with key themes discussed in the chapters, providing a hands-on approach to reflection, planning, and growth. Feel free to use them as often as you need. As your career evolves, these exercises can be used as your personal career toolkit, helping you adapt and refine the activities you have implemented from this workbook along the way.

Appendix A: Career Vision Board Exercise

Step 1: Brainstorm Your Vision

Start by identifying the words, phrases, or quotes that resonate with your career values and goals. Examples include leadership, innovation, growth, etc. Think about your idea of success and the key themes that inspire and motivate you. This exercise will help you clarify your vision before assembling your board.

Step 2: Create Your Mini Career Vision Board

Using the elements you have brainstormed, arrange and assemble them into a small, focused vision board that reflects your career aspirations. This mini vision board serves as a reference and source of inspiration as you navigate your professional path.

Appendix B: Career Vision Statement Template

A clear vision for your career can be a powerful guide, helping you make intentional decisions, stay motivated, and align your work with your values. The template below will help you articulate your ideal career in a way that is personal, inspiring, and actionable. As you fill it out, envision your future self—what excites you, what drives you, and what legacy you hope to leave behind. This statement is not set in stone; it can evolve as you grow and gain new experiences.

"In my ideal career, I am _____ (role/identity) who is known for _____ (values/strengths). I wake up each day feeling _____ (emotions) because I am engaged in _____ (work that excites you). I am constantly evolving by _____ (learning/growth activities), and I am mastering _____ (skills/knowledge). My work allows me to contribute by _____ (impact or legacy), and I want to be remembered for _____ (lasting contribution)."

Appendix C: Resources for Achieving SMART Objectives

As you develop your career action plan, it's essential to identify the resources needed to complete each step effectively. These resources aren't always external—often, they exist within our own networks. A Career Network Map serves as a powerful tool to visualize and evaluate the relationships that can support our professional goals. By mapping our network, we gain a high-level view of our connections, revealing opportunities for mentorship, job referrals, collaboration, and guidance.

Success is often tied to the people we are connected to through common interests, industries, or communities. A Career Network Map highlights the importance of these relationships and helps us strategically leverage our connections to navigate career opportunities.

C.1. What Is a Career Network Map?

A Career Network Map is a visual representation of your professional and personal connections. It provides insights into who is in your network, how they are connected to you, and where opportunities may exist. More than just a contact list, this map categorizes relationships into groups, making it easier to identify which individuals can support specific aspects of your career development.

For example, you may discover:

- A former colleague who can introduce you to a hiring manager at your dream company.
- A mentor who offers guidance on career growth.
- A community organization that provides leadership opportunities.
- A friend who works in a field you are interested in transitioning into.

By understanding these relationships in a structured way, you can identify gaps, strengthen weak ties, and build strategic connections that align with your career goals.

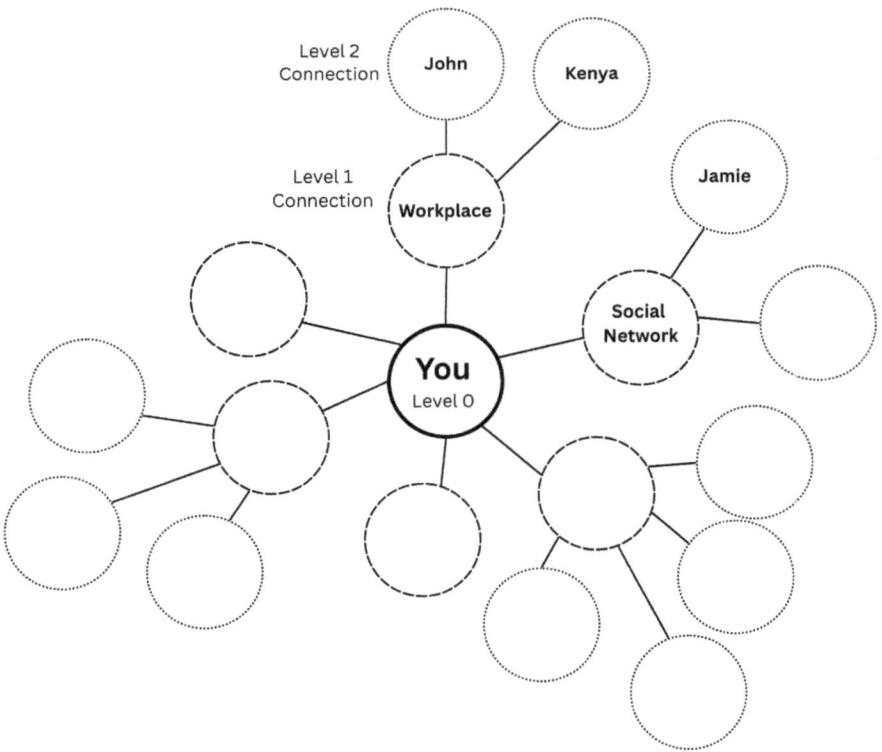

How to Create Your Career Network Map

When thinking about our network, we often recall people individually, which can lead to inconsistency and overlooked connections. Instead, it's more effective to think in groups—this makes it easier to systematically identify all key relationships. Like the illustration below, you are going to create your own Career Network Map.

Step-by-Step Guide to Creating a Career Network Map

Step 1: Place Yourself at the Center (Level 0)

- Begin by drawing yourself in the middle of your map.
- You are the nucleus, and your connections will expand outward.

Step 2: Identify Your Core Network Groups (Level 1)

- Around your name, draw primary network groups—broad categories that represent different areas of your life.
- Examples of Level 1 groups include:
    - Workplace Connections (e.g., colleagues, managers, clients)
    - Educational Network (e.g., professors, classmates, alumni)
    - Professional Associations (e.g., industry groups, trade organizations)
    - Mentors & Sponsors (e.g., career mentors, executive sponsors)
    - Personal & Social Network (e.g., friends, family, social media contacts)
    - Community & Volunteer Groups (e.g., nonprofits, faith-based groups)
    - Online & Industry Contacts (e.g., LinkedIn, conference connections)

Step 3: Add Individual Connections (Level 2)

- Within each **Level 1 group**, list specific individuals you know.
- Be as thorough as possible—think of past and present relationships.
- For example, under "Workplace Connections," list your current and former managers, colleagues, and collaborators.

Step 4: Expand Your Map Further (Level 3 & Beyond)

- Some individuals in **Level 2** may have their own valuable networks that you can tap into.
- For example:
  - A former manager may connect you to industry leaders.
  - A college professor may introduce you to graduate programs or research opportunities.
  - A LinkedIn connection may refer you to a job opportunity in your target field.

Your Career Network Map can expand as deep as necessary to capture important relationships.

Use the box below to create your own Career Network Map.

Using a Career Network Map

Once your network is mapped, use it strategically to support your goals. It can be used to identify the right people for your goals (E.g., if you need a job referral, you can look at your workplace or alumni network groups, but exploring a career change may require that you reach out to your industry contacts or mentor and sponsor groups). Mapping your network also strengthens relations by reconnecting to colleagues and spotting gaps in your network if one group is less robust than the others. Like many templates in this workbook, the Career Network Map should be dynamic, making it a living document as you meet new people.

Think about your development action plan from Chapter 5 and how your network can help you.

Objective #1: _____

    Who can help? _____

    Action step: _____

Objective #2: _____

    Who can help? _____

    Action step: _____

Objective #3: _____

    Who can help? _____

    Action step: _____

Your network is one of the most valuable career assets you have. Building and maintaining strong connections can unlock opportunities, accelerate career growth, and provide support during transitions. The Career Network Map is not just an exercise—it's a strategic career tool that helps you take control of your professional relationships. As you work toward your goals, use your map to identify, leverage, and expand your network.

C.2. Action Plan Template for implementing SMART Objectives

This worksheet will help you outline clear and actionable steps to help you achieve your SMART objectives. For each objective, define the necessary tasks and actions, required resources, deadlines, and success metrics.

SMART Objective #1: _____

_____

Actionable Steps:

Task 1	
Task 2	
Task 3	

Resources Needed:

_____

_____

Due Date: _____

Success Metric:

_____

_____

_____

SMART Objective #2: _____

_____

Actionable Steps:

Task 1	
Task 2	
Task 3	

Resources Needed:

_____

_____

Due Date: _____

Success Metric:

_____

_____

_____

_____

_____

_____

SMART Objective #3: _____

_____

Actionable Steps:

Task 1	
Task 2	
Task 3	

Resources Needed:

_____

_____

Due Date: _____

Success Metric:

_____

_____

_____

_____

_____

_____

References

1. Murray, J. D., Bernacchia, A., Roy, N. A., Constantinidis, C., Romo, R., & Wang, X.-J. (2017). Stable population coding for working memory coexists with heterogeneous neural dynamics in prefrontal cortex. *Neuron, 95*(2), 460-473.e4. https://doi.org/10.1016/j.neuron.2017.06.025

2. Rhodes, J., Nedza, K., May, J., & Clements, L. (2024). Imagery training for athletes with low imagery abilities. *Journal of Applied Sport Psychology, 36*(5), 831–844. https://doi.org/10.1080/10413200.2024.2337019

3. Travers, M. (2024, March 29). A psychologist explains the power of vision boarding for success. *Forbes.* https://www.forbes.com/sites/traversmark/2024/03/29/a-psychologist-explains-the-power-of-vision-boarding-for-success/

4. Bailey C. Benedict (2021) Using Vision Boards to Reflect on Relevant Experiences and Envision Ideal Futures, College Teaching, 69:4, 231-232, DOI: 10.1080/87567555.2020.1850411

5. Sheeran, P., Klein, W. M. P., & Rothman, A. J. (2017). Health behavior change: Moving from observation to intervention. *Annual Review of Psychology, 68*, 573-600, https://doi.org/10.1016/j.jcps.2016.02.005

6. Bailey RR. Goal Setting and Action Planning for Health Behavior Change. Am J Lifestyle Med. 2017 Sep 13;13(6):615-618. doi: 10.1177/1559827617729634. PMID: 31662729; PMCID: PMC6796229.

7. Matthews, Gail, "The Impact of Commitment, Accountability, and Written Goals on Goal Achievement" (2007). Psychology | Faculty Presentations. 3. https://scholar.dominican.edu/psychology-faculty-conference-presentations/3

Notes

Notes

Notes

Acknowledgments

This workbook would not have been possible without the support of our family, mentors, and community; your unwavering support, encouragement, and belief in us have been foundational. Your support has fueled our passions and drive to create resources that empower others.

To our mentors—thank you for the wisdom, encouragement, and lessons that have shaped our perspectives. Your insights have enriched our collective journeys and, in turn, the pages of this workbook.

Like previous projects, this workbook started off as an idea, but once again, Mynd Matters Publishing instilled confidence and belief in the value this material can bring to readers. Thank you to this team for once again making it all a reality.

To the readers and participants who will engage with this content – thank you for trusting this process. Your dedication to your growth and success is the reason this work exists.

Finally, to everyone who has contributed, reviewed, and supported this project in big and small ways, your generosity and encouragement mean the world. *Visualize Your Professional Future* reflects collective wisdom, and we are deeply grateful.

www.ingramcontent.com/pod-product-compliance
Lightning Source LLC
Chambersburg PA
CBHW041145120626
46547CB00020B/3122